The Story

of

My Life

Created By

Dee Henderson

Copyright Notice

The Story

of

My Life

My Birth

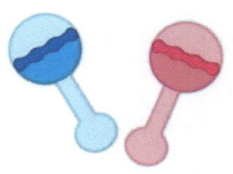

I was born on _____, _____,

at _____ o'clock in the _____.

The place I was born was _____,

located in _____.

I weighed _____.

My length was _____.

My Baby Photo

 # My Mom

My Dad

# My Brothers

My Sisters

# My Pets

My Home

My Aunts

My Uncles

My Grandmothers

My Grandfathers

My Childhood

# Photos and Ages

Young Adulthood

 # Photos and Ages

 Graduation

Date: _____

Time: _____

Where: _____

School: _____

Degree Program:

_____

 # Photos

# My Work

My Car

My Wedding

 Photos

Starting A Family

Children

Name

Birthdate

_____   _____

_____   _____

_____   _____

_____   _____

_____   _____

_____   _____

_____   _____

Photos of

My Sons

Photos of

My Daughters

Photos of

Our Pets

 Photos of

Our Home

 Special

Holidays

 Special

Holidays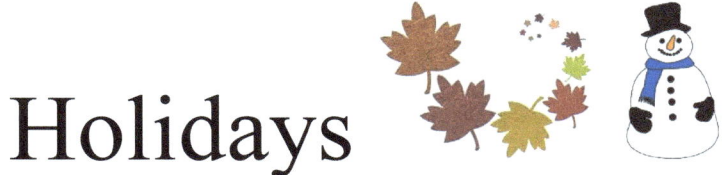

My Photo When I Became A Grandparent

 # My Grandchildren's Names and Birthdays

_____   _____

_____   _____

_____   _____

_____   _____

_____   _____

_____   _____

_____   _____

_____   _____

Photos of

My Grandsons

 # Photos of My

Granddaughters

Other Family Fun

And Good Times

 # More Family Fun

And Good Times

More Family Fun

And Good Times

More Family Fun

And Good Times

 # More Family Fun

And Good Times